AF382675

MANAGING ANXIETY AT WORK

Tips to beat stress, worry and panic

Written by Sabrina Biodore
Translated by Rebecca Neal

Coaching 50MINUTES.com

WORK WITHOUT STRESS AND WORRY

- **Problem:** how can you banish debilitating feelings of anxiety and panic?
- **Uses:** anxiety and panic are diffuse feelings which can seriously impact our personal and professional lives if they are left untreated.
- **Professional context:** wellbeing at work, stress management.
- **FAQs:**
  - What is the difference between anxiety and panic?
  - How can I identify the signs of anxiety?
  - How can I banish performance anxiety at work?
  - How does anxiety affect my professional performance?
  - What can happen if anxiety is left untreated?
  - What does a panic attack look like?
  - How can panic attacks hold me back at work?
  - How can homeopathy help with panic attacks?

Whether you are just starting out in your career or already have several years of professional experience under your belt, you no doubt share most people's desire for a relaxed atmosphere where you feel happy working, but where there are still enough challenges to keep you motivated. However, many of us feel unhappy or miserable at work; the growing number of articles on the subject published in newspapers and magazines attest to this.

What can you do when you find yourself feeling anxious on a daily basis, when worry and fear undermine your effectiveness or, even worse, when panic attacks leave you paralysed and unable to complete even the simplest tasks?

Anxiety is a major public health issue: in 2013, there were 8.2 million cases of anxiety reported in the UK, and women are around twice as likely as men to be diagnosed with an anxiety disorder. However, suffering from anxiety does not necessarily spell disaster: acting quickly and seeking appropriate medical and psychological care as soon as you identify persistent or recurring symptoms will allow you to treat these problems and significantly lessen their impact on your life.

In 50 minutes, this guide will show you the steps you can take on a daily basis to prevent these essentially minor problems from taking root, worsening or hampering your ability to fulfil your professional duties. Taking action before anxiety becomes debilitating will give you the best possible chance of overcoming it.

STRESS-FREE WORK: THE BASICS

SOME DEFINITIONS

Stress, anxiety and panic: what is the difference?

Work can be demanding, and the pressure it puts on us can leave us at risk of stress. However, before we begin, it is essential to distinguish between stress, anxiety and panic.

Stress refers to physical or psychological symptoms which appear in response to stimuli that are interpreted as sources of pressure, constraint or tension. Stress has many symptoms, and they vary from person to person, but some of the most common include vertigo, agitation and anxiety. Stress has physical, mental and behavioural effects.

Anxiety is characterised by temporary emotional disturbance. The individual experiences a sense of danger, which can vary in intensity and manifests itself through specific physical symptoms such as nerves, headaches, an elevated heart rate, stomach pain and insecurity. Anxiety is considered a normal response to stressful situations or real dangers, and allows us to deal with events and react appropriately. Anxiety becomes a problem when we suffer from it regularly for vague reasons with no precise cause, or when it becomes a permanent state.

Panic can be seen as the next step up from anxiety, meaning that a person who is regularly or permanently anxious is at risk of suffering from panic attacks. In this situation, they will feel a sense of impending doom and find themselves paralysed by fear. The symptoms of panic attacks include a feeling of impending death, a racing heartbeat, abdominal pain, a feeling of going mad, trembling and muscle spasms.

Definitions

Stress	
Definition	All the physical, psychological and behavioural symptoms which emerge in response to situations that cause a feeling of constraint or tension in the individual.
Symptoms (depending on the individual)	• Sweating • Vertigo • Agitation • Difficulty breathing

Anxiety	
Definition	Temporary emotional disturbance. Normal reaction to danger or stressful situations. Anxiety disorder refers to cases where the feeling of danger or stress is vague and has no apparent cause.
Symptoms (depending on the individual)	<u>Feeling of danger</u> • Stomach pain • Nerves • Elevated heart rate • Sweating • Headaches

Panic	
Definition	A step up from anxiety. Anxiety is uncontrolled and appears more regularly. Risk of panic attacks.
Symptoms (depending on the individual)	<u>Feeling of impending death</u> • Chest pain • Feeling of going mad • Stomach pain • Elevated heart rate • Muscle spasms

Anxiety and panic, which are already debilitating in themselves, can also develop into other, more serious illnesses, including generalised anxiety disorder (GAD), phobias, panic disorder and obsessive-compulsive disorder (OCD). They should therefore not be taken lightly: if you are affected by them, consult a specialist and begin treatment as soon as possible.

Performance anxiety

The demands of the modern working world, employees' desire to achieve, and the idea of "having it all" and succeeding at everything we do have led to new problems known as occupational stress. These new demands have generated performance anxiety in many workers, as they want to perform at their best at all times. However, it has been observed that constantly setting ever-higher objectives is actually counterproductive for workers, as these self-imposed challenges can have negative consequences.

Perfectionism and the desire to do well can help drive us forward. However, when employees put too much pressure on themselves to achieve results, in addition to the pressure coming from their managers, this can hamper their professional efforts. The monumental scope of their task and their constant dissatisfaction with themselves result in a vicious circle, as they become anxious, fear failure or feel that they are never good enough. This then leads to a loss of motivation, a decline in their capacities and, in the worst-case scenario, burnout. Burnout is an increasingly common phenomenon, and refers to total professional exhaustion: the employee is physically and mentally overwhelmed, and finds themselves unable to keep going. This is why it is so important to keep work in perspective: doing your tasks correctly is more than enough, and keeping extreme perfectionism and unattainable goals to a minimum is vital.

WHAT CAUSES ANXIETY AND PANIC?

Anxiety and panic do not have a single, specific cause. These irrational fears can emerge during childhood development, or following a traumatic incident at any period in life. There are therefore a number of environmental, medical and psychological factors behind anxiety disorders and panic attacks.

Environmental causes

Individuals may be more prone to anxiety disorders if they grew up in an unstable environment with anxious or abusive parents. Indeed, children who are regularly bullied or belittled are likely to struggle with self-esteem, and may also tend to worry excessively about completely harmless situations. Conversely, anxiety can also be passed on by overprotective parents, who see danger everywhere and transmit their worries to their child. When the child becomes an adult, they may be more likely to suffer from generalised anxiety, anxiety disorders or phobias.

Medical causes

Some illnesses, such as diabetes, asthma, heart disease and thyroid disorders (which affect the endocrine gland at the base of the neck) cause symptoms similar to those which occur during anxiety attacks: breathing difficulties, chest pains, stomach pains, sweating, and so on. These illnesses also generally influence mood and stress levels.

Consequently, if you regularly experience mood swings or irrational anxiety, it is essential to begin by ruling out any possible biological or medical causes. Your GP will be able to prescribe the appropriate tests and carry out a detailed physical examination. Eliminating other diagnoses will allow you to be sure that you are really suffering from anxiety.

Psychological causes

Everyday events affect different people in different ways, depending on their upbringing, environment and formative experiences.

Anxiety issues can be triggered by a traumatic event such as a physical assault, the loss of a loved one, an accident or a natural disaster. Fear of reliving the traumatic situation can lead to avoidant behaviour that the individual cannot control and which makes their daily life extremely difficult.

PTSD OR ANXIETY?

It is essential to distinguish between post-traumatic stress disorder (PTSD), a feeling of intense shock that appears shortly after traumatic incidents and generally goes away after a few months, and anxiety disorders, which stem from the same kind of event and can take root for good if they are not treated promptly and effectively.

This kind of problem can also be caused by a desire to always perform at your best at work, a fear of being replaced or a fear of ending up unemployed. In this case, anxiety and panic can lead to problems in your working relationships, which will in turn negatively impact your professional life.

CONSEQUENCES ON DAY-TO-DAY AND PROFESSIONAL LIFE

Managing your anxiety issues can soon turn into a daily nightmare. The physical symptoms outlined earlier (palpitations, breathing difficulties, and so on) can be debilitating and demand immediate, potentially time-consuming care in order to be temporarily calmed. Understandably, this can pose problems in any situation.

Furthermore, the recurrence of these symptoms can cause or exacerbate a range of illnesses. Palpitations, chest pains and other symptoms can lead to heart problems such as high blood pressure and angina, and even to heart attacks (for example during a panic attack). Stress, which will spike if you are constantly anxious, can result in ulcers or hormonal issues (such as disruptions in cortisol secretion). These secondary illnesses can be attributed to anxiety-related problems. People struggling with anxiety may also suffer from headaches and sleep disturbances.

In the world of work, panic attacks can stop employees from carrying out their tasks, and anxiety and panic both interfere with efficiency. These problems can also harm professional relationships, as anxious people may be irritable or uncomfortable around their colleagues, which will affect the working environment. Performance anxiety may further exacerbate existing difficulties.

What is more, if anxiety is not treated promptly, sufferers may sink into depression or take refuge in alcohol or drug abuse.

The most important thing is to take action and to know that the situation is far from hopeless. Fortunately, there are a range of treatments for anxiety and panic, so you can find the best solution for you. Do not wait to seek help!

OVERCOMING ANXIETY AND PANIC

Anxiety and panic can be diagnosed if symptoms have been present for at least six months and any underlying illnesses have been ruled out following a medical consultation.

Treatment is based on both medication and psychological care. Relaxing activities which relieve stress are also highly recommended and can help to lessen the problem.

Medical treatment

The main medications used to treat anxiety are:

- **Antidepressants**, which can lessen anxiety by influencing neurotransmitters (chemical elements which are synthesised by neurones and which affect the transmission of nerve impulses).
- **Anxiolytics**, such as benzodiazepines (including Xanax, Tranxene and Lysanxia), which lessen the feelings linked to anxiety problems or stop symptoms from emerging. The major disadvantage of anxiolytics such as benzodiazepines is that they are potentially addic-

tive. It is therefore essential to follow the prescribed course of treatment and avoid stopping suddenly. Doctors typically prescribe a two- or three-month course of anxiolytics in order to assess the effectiveness of the treatment. If you plan on stopping, you should discuss this with your doctor first and stop gradually (reduction of the dose under supervision in order to prevent withdrawal symptoms). Anxiolytics have been proven to have a significant impact on the symptoms of anxiety, and patients tend to feel calmer quickly.

Psychological treatment

Medication is used to treat the manifestations of anxiety and panic, not their causes. These causes can be treated with psychological care. Therapy is therefore the first-line treatment for anxiety and panic, since without it we can only eradicate the symptoms and not the root causes.

Therapy will allow the patient to first of all identify the psychological causes of their problems, before examining the mechanisms behind them. This will in turn enable them to modify these mechanisms and deal with anxious episodes effectively. There are a range of types of therapy:

- In **psychoanalytic therapy**, the patient attends sessions with a trained therapist and learns to deal with their symptoms and problems by talking about them and putting them into words. The patient freely associates objects, places and events from their past and links them to their current problems. They dissect the different periods of their life, from infancy to adulthood, that could be at the root of their problems. Determining the factors behind anxiety problems makes it possible to take action and find the right treatment for each individual's situation.
- **Cognitive behavioural therapy** (CBT) takes place over a fixed, relatively short period of time (generally between three and six months). When used alongside antidepressants, CBT can prevent relapses. It has a very specific aim: it allows the patient (with the help of the therapist) to identify the problematic behaviour they use to deal with particular situations. This means that CBT is an ideal way of correcting behaviour resulting from generalised anxiety disorder. During sessions,

the patient describes episodes of anxiety or panic and their symptoms, and looks at the ways they deal with these episodes (avoidance, self-defeating behaviour, and so on). The therapist then helps them to "reprogramme" these behaviours so that they can respond better to challenging events in future. For example, if you are terrified of public speaking and always manage to delegate this task to someone else, the therapist will help you to understand where this anxiety comes from. They will then help you to work on the responses you have developed by examining the reasons behind them: why do I delegate this task to someone else? Why do I think I cannot do it? How can I speak in public successfully? This type of exercise will enable you to speak in front of a group, and even to lead a meeting. CBT is also used to treat obsessive-compulsive disorder, eating disorders such as anorexia and bulimia, and depression.

Prevention

Relaxing activities can be very beneficial in combatting the stress that precedes anxiety, whether they are used alongside other treatments or as a preventative measure:

- **Relaxation techniques** are sometimes used during CBT to help the patient to relax. When an individual is struggling with repetitive, intrusive thoughts, relaxation techniques can help them to switch off from their everyday worries and reduce their stress levels by influencing the physical manifestations of stress: lower heart rate, relaxed muscles, fewer thoughts, and so on. The benefits of this approach are very clear. There are a range of different relaxation techniques, including abdominal breathing, sophrology, self-hypnosis, yoga and aromatherapy, and they can be used both as part of anxiety treatment and independently of it.
- Regular **exercise** is another way of combatting anxiety and panic attacks, as it is a good outlet for any tension the individual may be experiencing. After just 30 minutes of physical activity, the body releases endorphins, which

are hormones linked to wellbeing. Endorphins are responsible for the feeling of relaxation and contentment we feel after exercise, which means that they help to improve our day-to-day wellbeing.

You will get even better results if you make sure that you are getting plenty of sleep and make time for activities that allow you to recharge your batteries (spending time with your family, going for a walk in the countryside, meeting up with friends, and so on). Since our digestive system also plays a vital role in our overall wellbeing, eating a healthy, balanced diet and avoiding harmful substances such as coffee, tobacco and alcohol is also essential.

TEN ANXIETY-BUSTING FOODS

As long as they are eaten in moderation (as with everything), some foods are known for their beneficial effects on the nervous system. These include:

- probiotics, which can be found in yo-ghurts, among other sources;
- oily fish, such as salmon, sardines and

trout;
* wholegrain cereals;
* bananas;
* blueberries;
* eggs;
* seagrasses;
* almonds;
* chocolate;
* green or camomile tea.

There is a lot of truth in the old saying "healthy mind in a healthy body", so these seemingly obvious points are still essential when it comes to treating anxiety and panic. Dealing with these problems will allow you to work more effectively, enjoy your work more, maintain good relationships with your colleagues and be your best, highest-performing and most effective self.

SUMMARY

The length of treatment for anxiety- and panic-related illnesses will vary from person to person, depending on the seriousness of the problem. There are many ways of treating these issues, including medication (anxiolytics and antidepressants) and therapy (psychoanalytic therapy and cognitive behavioural therapy). Relaxing activities such as sport and relaxation exercises complement this treatment and can eliminate or significantly lessen the symptoms of these debilitating illnesses. This means that you do not have to simply put up with anxiety and panic.

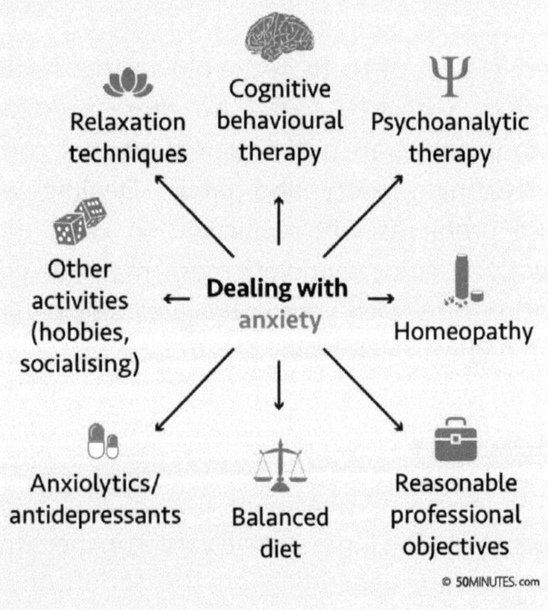

TOP TIPS

- Make sure you can distinguish between work-related stress and stress linked to your daily life, and between temporary anxiety (which is normal), pathological anxiety (which has no apparent cause and has unmanageable symptoms lasting at least six months), and generalised anxiety (which is characterised by a feeling of imminent danger and excessive, debilitating fear).
- Start by consulting a doctor to rule out any possible biological causes for your symptoms (diabetes, heart conditions, hyperthyroidism, asthma, and so on).
- If your symptoms do not go away, take action as soon as possible. The sooner you start treatment, the fewer episodes of severe anxiety you are likely to experience. Ignoring the problem will only make it worse.
- If your problems do not have a biological cause and are intense, frequent or constant, and if you are suffering from anxiety attacks, panic attacks, OCD or irrational phobias, you should

consider psychological treatment. This can be accompanied by medication to help you relax.

- A healthy lifestyle will enable you to handle all your activities effectively. Eat balanced meals, exercise, go to bed at a similar time every day and make sure you get enough rest. These basic precautions work for everyone and will enable you to face pressure at work with aplomb.
- If you are naturally stressed in your everyday life, this is liable to have an impact on your professional life. Finding ways to unwind (such as going for a jog, swimming, doing yoga or getting a massage) will allow you to curb episodes of generalised anxiety. Opt for a sport or another activity that lets you relax and feel comfortable in your own skin.
- Some plants, including hops, passionflower and valerian, have relaxing properties. Drinking herbal or fruit teas (for example in the evening before you go to bed) can help you to feel calm and relaxed. In less severe cases of anxiety, over-the-counter remedies containing extracts of these plants may be helpful.

FAQS

WHAT IS THE DIFFERENCE BETWEEN ANXIETY AND PANIC?

Anxiety is a normal reaction to stressful events (such as the approach of an important deadline) or difficult situations (such as a driving test or a presentation at work). It causes a feeling of apprehension which enables the subject to respond to the situation. It stops being normal when it emerges without an identifiable cause and lasts for a long time.

Panic is an acute manifestation of anxiety. Individuals suffering from panic experience repeated, apparently unprovoked episodes of total malaise, with symptoms including irrational fear, a feeling of impending death, palpitations, sweating and nausea.

HOW CAN I IDENTIFY THE SIGNS OF ANXIETY?

There are many signs of anxiety, which vary from person to person. However, certain symptoms are shared by many anxiety sufferers and may indicate that all is not well:

- you constantly or frequently feel worried even in the absence of stressful situations;
- you are irritable and constantly tired;
- your heart races for no reason, you have difficulty breathing, you sweat a lot, or you have chest or stomach pains;
- you suffer from nausea or sudden headaches.

If you experience several of these symptoms on repeated occasions, accompanied by a vague feeling of worry that lasts for several months, you are almost certainly suffering from anxiety or panic. This means it is now time to consult a doctor.

HOW CAN I BANISH PERFORMANCE ANXIETY AT WORK?

Wanting to be up to the job, perform well and do good work are all positive goals that should motivate you in your work. However, when the bar is set too high or workers are under too much pressure, anxiety can set in. You can curb performance anxiety by ensuring that work does not take priority over all other areas of your life and that you do not focus on it at the expense of sleep or exercise. Setting moderate but still rewarding objectives and paying attention to your wellbeing can prevent performance anxiety from rearing its head.

HOW DOES ANXIETY AFFECT MY PROFESSIONAL PERFORMANCE?

Anxiety has a range of consequences on your professional life: it can leave you feeling irritable or tense with your colleagues or your work, cause you to struggle to concentrate on and complete certain tasks, inspire panic and leave you flustered (for example if you are in charge of organising a meeting), and cause you to develop coping mechanisms, such as avoiding challenging situations.

WHAT CAN HAPPEN IF ANXIETY IS LEFT UNTREATED?

If anxiety is not treated, it can become chronic and result in unmanageable, persistent symptoms. It can also develop into:

- Generalised anxiety disorder (GAD), when anxiety becomes more or less permanent. Sufferers feel worried about a number of things across various areas of their life.
- Anxiety or panic attacks, meaning episodes in which the suffer experiences intense symptoms of anxiety. In these situations, the person is paralysed by fear and feels as though they are about to die. Some individuals also hyperventilate (meaning that their breathing becomes faster and deeper) during panic attacks.
- Phobias, such as social phobia, which denotes an irrational fear of all interactions with others, or agoraphobia, which refers to a fear of being in public places that are difficult to escape from. Agoraphobics are afraid that

they will not be able to get help immediately should the need arise. As we can see, phobias can take many forms.

- Obsessive-compulsive disorder (OCD). OCD involves compulsively repeating the same gestures in a given situation, which is the sufferer's way of dealing with a situation that causes anxiety for them.

WHAT DOES A PANIC ATTACK LOOK LIKE?

Panic attacks are disruptive, debilitating episodes. During panic attacks, sufferers feel afraid, panicked and as though they might be dying, and are completely unable to manage the episode. Symptoms include sweating, stomach or chest pains, an elevated heart rate and nausea. During the attack, irrational fear is exacerbated by a feeling of total loss of control. When this happens at work, the person will be temporarily incapacitated, which may be difficult to deal with and can cause painful feelings of embarrassment in addition to the stress that accompanies the episode.

HOW CAN PANIC ATTACKS HOLD ME BACK AT WORK?

Panic attacks are acute, intense episodes that take place when the individual's response mechanisms are overwhelmed. They are then completely unable to react to the situation, and during some episodes with particularly severe symptoms, medical treatment may be necessary.

If panic attacks become too numerous and too frequent, the individual will be completely unable to carry out their work for an indefinite period of time. In this case, a temporary break or even a long spell away from work may be necessary so that suitable treatment can be administered. Obviously, this will subsequently hold the person back professionally.

HOW CAN HOMEOPATHY HELP WITH PANIC ATTACKS?

Some homeopathic remedies can be used to combat anxiety and panic. These include Gelsemium 9CH, which works best as a background treatment, Aconitum Napellus 15 to 30CH, which is used to treat panic attacks, and Ambra Grisea 15CH, which can lessen heart palpitations caused by anxiety and panic. This list is far from exhaustive, and it is highly recommended to discuss your situation with a doctor before starting any treatment.

OVER TO YOU

Are you already familiar with laughter yoga? This approach is based on the widely accepted fact that laughter is good for you: among other benefits, it drives away anxiety for a least a short while, beginning as soon as you start laughing. Laughter yoga is also based on another observation: our brains cannot tell the difference between spontaneous laughter inspired by a funny situation and voluntary laughter with no particular cause. The exercises below will allow you to generate genuine happiness simply by using your facial muscles.

START THE DAY WITH A LAUGH

This exercise should be practised as often as possible, so that ideally it will become a reflex, like brushing your teeth, no matter how busy or difficult the day ahead of you.

- Start by smiling at your reflection in the mirror. Then turn your smile into a frown, before letting your imagination run wild: frown, grimace, open your eyes wide, scowl, stick your tongue out, and so on.

- When you take a shower, force yourself to laugh and sing, without taking yourself too seriously. Even better, force yourself to sing out of tune, especially if you have a good voice.
- Once you have showered and dressed, stand in front of the mirror again and try to charm yourself. Try out an intense gaze, a captivating smile or a seductive pout, then laugh again at your faces.

If you live with other people (roommates, partner, children, and so on), feel free to include them in your funny faces or seductive expressions – but maybe not every morning!

SMILING MEDITATION

If funny faces are not for you, or if you want to try a complementary exercise at another time of day (in the evening before you go to bed, for example), opt for smiling meditation. Sit on a chair with your back straight and your feet planted firmly on the floor. Close your eyes, take a few deep breaths and listen to your breathing until you feel calm. Then bring to mind a situation, image or memory that makes you happy and smile. Keep focusing on this image, breathing deeply and smiling, and feel the happiness flood your heart and body. Try to hold onto this feeling for a few minutes before opening your eyes again.

RELAXED PRESENTATIONS

Just before you give a presentation, try to find an isolated place where other people cannot see or hear you. Stand up and lean forward, and start to imitate loud, violent, body-shaking sobs. Then straighten up slowly and gradually replace tears with increasingly loud theatrical laughter (ho ho ho, ha ha ha, hee hee hee). When your back is fully straight and your head is up, raise your arms above your head and burst out laughing.

Feel free to go through this exercise several times before you have to speak in public, as it should allow you to let go of tension.

FURTHER READING

BIBLIOGRAPHY

- AXA Prévention. (No date) *Comprendre et traiter l'anxiété.* [Online]. [Accessed 5 October 2017]. Available from: <https://www.axaprevention.fr/sante-bien-etre/sante-question/anxiete>

- Baker, R. (2011) *Understanding Panic Attacks and Overcoming Fear.* Oxford: Lion Hudson.

- Brodar, C. (2012) La crise d'angoisse : comment calmer ses angoisses ? *Passeport Santé.* [Online]. [Accessed 5 October 2017]. Available from: <http://www.passeport-sante.net/fr/Maux/Problemes/Fiche.aspx?doc=attaque_de_panique_pm>

- Cornette de Saint-Cyr, X. and Poisson, M. (2014) *Sortir de l'anxiété. Mode d'emploi.* Chêne-Bourg, Switzerland: Éditions Jouvence.

- Duchène, C. (No date) Quand l'anxiété devient une maladie. *Doctissimo.* [Online]. [Accessed 5 October 2017]. Available from: <http://www.doctissimo.fr/html/psychologie/stress_angoisse/ps_2573_anxiete_maladie.htm>

- EurekaSanté. (2015) *Anxiéte.* [Online]. [Accessed 5 October 2017]. Available from: <https://eureka-

sante.vidal.fr/maladies/psychisme/anxiete.html>

- Gruyer, A. and Sidhoum, K. (2015) Thérapie comportementale et cognitive (TCC). *Psycom.* [Online]. [Accessed 5 October 2017]. Available from: <http://www.psycom.org/Soins-accompagnements-et-entraide/Therapies/Therapie-comportementale-et-cognitive-TCC>

- Hordé, P. (2017) Homéopathie contre l'angoisse et la nervosité. *Le journal des femmes.* [Online]. [Accessed 5 October 2017]. Available from: <http://sante-medecine.journaldesfemmes.com/contents/856-homeopathie-contre-l-angoisse-et-la-nervosite>

- Maillard, C. (2012) Les thérapies cognitives et comportementales. *Psychologies.* [Online]. [Accessed 5 October 2017]. Available from: <http://www.psychologies.com/Therapies/Toutes-les-therapies/Psychotherapies/Articles-et-Dossiers/Les-therapies-cognitives-et-comportementales>

- Maillard, C. (2009). La souffrance au travail : la fin d'un tabou. *Doctissimo.* [Online]. [Accessed 5 October 2017]. Available from: <http://www.doctissimo.fr/html/psychologie/stress_angoisse/articles/13942-souffrance-travail.htm>

- Mental Health Foundation. (No date) *Mental health statistics: anxiety.* [Online]. [Accessed 5 October 2017]. Available from: <https://www.mentalhealth.org.uk/statistics/mental-health-statistics-anxiety>

- Pons, G. (2017) La relaxation. *Doctissimo.* [Online]. [Accessed 5 October 2017]. Available from: <http://www.doctissimo.fr/html/forme/rem_forme/fo_1116_relaxation.htm>

- Senk, P. (2013) En finir avec l'anxiété de perfor-mance. *Le Figaro.* [Online]. [Accessed 5 October 2017]. Available from: <http://sante.lefigaro.fr/actualite/2013/03/15/20070-finir-avec-lan-xiete-performance>

- Seugon, A. (No date) Angoisse et anxiété. *Doctissimo.* [Online]. [Accessed 5 October 2017]. Available from: <http://www.doctissimo.fr/html/psychologie/stress_angoisse/ps_1515_an-goisse_anx.htm>

ADDITIONAL SOURCES

- Edelman, S. (2006) *Change Your Thinking with CBT: Overcome Stress, Combat Anxiety and Improve Your Life.* London: Vermilion.

- O'Morain, P. (2016) *Mindfulness for Worriers: Overcome Everyday Stress and Anxiety.* London: Hodder & Stoughton.

- Plant, J. and Stephenson, J. (2011) *Beating Stress, Anxiety and Depression: Groundbreaking ways to help you feel better.* London: Piaktus Books.

- Radomme, B. (2017) *Overcoming Anxiety.* Trans. Neal, R. Brussels: Plurilingua Publishing.

IMPROVE YOUR GENERAL KNOWLEDGE

IN A BLINK OF AN EYE !

www.50minutes.com